The Anti-Grief

The Anti-Grief

MARIANNE BORUCH

COPPER CANYON PRESS

PORT TOWNSEND, WASHINGTON

Cover art: Young Sun Han, *Ghost Complex 1*, 2013. Archival Inkjet print,
36 x 24 inches (914 x 610 mm)

Copper Canyon Press is in residence at Fort Worden State Park in
Port Townsend, Washington, under the auspices of Centrum.
Centrum is a gathering place for artists and creative thinkers
from around the world, students of all ages and backgrounds,
and audiences seeking extraordinary cultural enrichment.

LIBRARY OF CONGRESS CATALOGING-IN-PUBLICATION DATA
Names: Boruch, Marianne, 1950– author.
Title: The anti-grief / Marianne Boruch.
Description: Port Townsend, Washington : Copper Canyon Press, [2019]
Identifiers: LCCN 2019013489 | ISBN 9781556595684 (pbk. : alk. paper)
Classification: LCC PS3552.O75645 A6 2019 | DDC 811/.54—dc23
LC record available at https://lccn.loc.gov/2019013489

9 8 7 6 5 4 3 2 FIRST PRINTING

COPPER CANYON PRESS
Post Office Box 271
Port Townsend, Washington 98368
www.coppercanyonpress.org

Sometimes our hearts are stone. Sometimes not.

BRIGIT PEGEEN KELLY

CONTENTS

The Anti-Grief

Pieces on the Ground

I gave up the pencil, the walk in woods, the fog
at dawn, a keyhole I lost an eye to.

And the habit of early, of acorn into oak—
    bent   tangled   choked because of ache or greed,
    or lousy light deemed it so.

So what. Give up that so what.

O fellow addicts of the arch and the tragic, give up
    the thousand-pound *if* and *when* too.
    Give up whatever made the bed or unmade it.

Give up the know thing that shatters into other things
    and takes the remember fork in the road.

The remember isn't a road.

At noon, the fog has no memory of fog, the trees I walked
    or wanted to. Like the pencil never recalls its least
    little mark, the dash loved, the comma that can't,

can *not* dig down what its own brief nothing
    means on the page. I don't understand death either.

By afternoon, the brain is box, is breath let go, a kind of
    mood music agog, half emptied by the usual
    who am I, who are you, who's anyone.

Truth is, I listen all night for morning, all day
    for night in the trees draped like a sound I never quite

get how it goes. There's a phantom self, nerved-up
    as any missing arm or leg.

Of course I was. Of course I stared from the yard,
    my mother at the window

rinsing knife and spoon and the middle of her life.

In drawing class, all eyes fix on the figure gone
    imaginary, thinning to paper. Not the wind or a cry

how the hand makes, our bent to it

—pause and rush, rush and pause—

small animals heard only at night, spooked in the leaves.

Θ

Salmon

How salmon love
sex enough to fight uphill in waters blasting
brilliant, some
one hundred mph (fact-checkers,
forget it, I'm close). How we stood, old inkling
of such exhausting *omg*, Darwin
would have... (the difference, same-
thingness, animal hungers and fury and persistence,
some amazing *something next*)
exploded!—his head
on a pillow most afternoons in the parlor, wrapped
in her quiet concern. Emma, the perfect nurse, they say,
who married the perfect patient,
Victorian fable, velvet-striped wallpaper even
on the ceiling would be my guess.
Because that trip he took in youth is
everlasting youth, island of
huge tortoises and the tiny cactus finch
plus his other
green spot in the sea, its DNA trace
of the grand extinct dodo
too trusting to run from sailors with their clubs, too weird
and bigger, certainly more
feathered and blank-eyed than one impossible
irreplaceable Great Uncle Cedric
I heard of, just wanting a little honest-to-god
barbecue at the wedding.
The forces of life
are mysterious. But thrilling
and painful, August in Alaska near
Seward, gone up in a firestorm during
the quake, 1964, any year in a fade next to our
stunned standing at the salmon weir,
a patch of woods, sunlit river
raging, those bright muscle-creatures blown back
at it at it leaping, failing spectacular
upstarts all over again
human. What it means to
love is speechless.

The Museum of Silence

Those Poor Clares must wonder why the racket

louder than usual, three-euros-a-pop
tourists queueing up outside,
weekends the convent on pause.

It's the noise in their heads, the old nun
might say with what's left
in her head, the girlhood part: war,

a low-flying plane, the loud, hoarse agony

of cows shattered from above into petal by
red petal, garish sprays in grass
north of these olive groves.

(Museum of Silence as secret or
scent, day of misjudgment,
Italy, the baffling website, our

stop-start train to Fara Sabina.)

Quiet is what's *after*, the old nun
tells the young nun who has
an edge, that eye thing, she has a look.

This too I invent: is it vanity or just
the old woman in wonder, going on
so vividly the long-ago boy in that cockpit

can't even have a thought, he's so scared.

And the younger nun: So now it's
forgive us *their* trespasses?
Not out loud. In her head. Belief can narrow

for good like that. What's left is
a lever, a simple jack of amazement to
pry open the very first museum on earth,

a sanctuary for the muses.

Of course. From the Greek *μουσεῖον*,
part cemetery. Latin's closer,
mūsēum, its small banquet room to keep

the dead living, a spot for reverent
frolic and grief. The Ancients
mourn, loving the lost off to their

out-of-body nowhere or somewhere,

eating with them one last time.
The original church-basement lunch
after the funeral, I suppose.

And those ladies who
toil among the fruit salad, ham spread,
the muted voices—

O long-robed muses of oldest days,

(for Poetry lyric and epic and sacred,
for Music, History, Dance, et al) come hither!
Even you, wordless stricken one

called Tragedy, the *start over,*
dark forever thus
in such places, that bright

moth bitten-blind ring of leaves you wear.

May Day

The child, the miniature
old person waiting in her was worry,
all that sitting alone in a tree thinking the tree
knew her thoughts.

Walking home, just walking like that...

A kind of radar. It does ache,
scanning the waters *Is*
turning to *Was* turned to who can recall
the inch-by-inch days of school.
What got learned piled up or it morphed
to the next thing and left behind

a little smoke.

There are children with
no child inside. But here's a bird for you, says Spring,
brought back from the dead of

snow and ice. Plus flowers, the first blue (sweet
low-to-the-ground vinca), first yellow
(forsythia's wild reach every which way).
And those hearts in the garden again, their red
and their white bleed so meticulously

minting sorrow—classic, ridiculous, too many—

one might think them fake, stamped out in some factory
an ocean away, two continents. A good third of
the workers underage, trying so hard.

That Thing

I have a lot of rue in me.

A bicycle tire to fix.
World peace to attend to.
Bones in the x-ray not lighting up right.

I have an ear
for that scratching in the wall that
keeps one awake in the short run,
like: whether to tell you
that thing or not.

That thing. So many names for it but certain
categories in the subset of
small and dark include
all the better to see you with, my dear, said the wolf
in that bonnet swiped from
the grandmother he ate. Try to figure a logic there
if you come into the story midway. Which
is every human's condition.

Case in point: my family's ridiculous habit,
showing up to movies halfway through. Then sitting
the same mileage into the next run—
theaters couldn't care less, all day if you wanted—
until scenes got familiar, a runaway train, a kitchen knife
redropped. Until my mother, reduced
to a whisper: *this is where we came in* meant
finish your popcorn, we're going.

If I told you
the screw-up, the backstory
of that thing I should
tell you… Ugh. Such earnestness in the world
is exhausting. Consider the local Y, full up
with the breathless on machines,
persistent perfect shapes-to-be while
the youngest among us sit poolside, stunned
to a rivet by a crushing coach.
Look at my nose! shouts the bellowed monster of the shallows.
Their little heads turn.

To sleep is to dream all the way. But too much
of that thing went on today.

I lower my head to the pillow for my brain
to be washed all night—
Because you said
that happens, that's the drill. Whatever fluids
I had no part in making

run ragtag and rivered over my
bleak-in-there, for hours.

A Rescue

The whale might, she might vaguely recognize
human cries of those drowning

as some distant tribe of fin
and blowhole. And the damaged

submarine, her cousin once   twice
three times removed, huge and gray

in the blood-let Atlantic's notorious
cold beyond cold lined at bottom with

outrageous fish whose photos in a glossy
seasick book could wide-eye you

to some moon creature,
their razors on stalks bright-blinking

right off their heads to terrify or protect.
So the great species of the planet

unite underwater where we earth-stuck
oxygen eaters rarely look or think to look.

And on hearing those cries—
Wait, doesn't the whale have a massive

mammal heart, a child could
run through it. That sound, such a flood

to the brain. (Brain curious as a calf in spring
folded up, tangled, still wet

from the going.) *Do something!* billows
and bells through the hopeless

slate-blue. The whale's identical first
cell of us too in that watery void before

we turned sea creature here,
land breather there, damned the same to

archangel across, down deepest
lost. Stunned ocean. Unquiet.

Wound

I found a paper ruler made
to measure one exact. Up to six inches or
in centimeters, take your pick.
A little worn and bent
in one place. Now on a shelf on its
calibrated edge. Imagine
the ambulance, an EMT close, reading
tiny print. *Discard*

after single use. And I wonder
if shattered glass and smoking engine
got in the of rescue, whether
the wound one inch or two, if the jagged fleshy depth
really a trapdoor the spirit took
to leave the body for good.

I have a kit in my car, a zippered black bag of
bandages and ointment, a knife, scissors in there,
and inexplicitly, rope—what else—

Endless gauze. A waterfall of gauze, a frozen field
of gauze but soft, the opposite of chain mail
knights wore into battle, told
sure, every fight is noble. But even history forgets
why oh why oh why.

Blood-rush. Garish shock of
alive! escape! An ambulance fact sheet says
abridgment, says a complete
exorcism—did I read that right?—of exposed edges.
Bleeding, stop. Wound, begin to close—

Promise and threat go on because one
has to prophesy
to make any sense of tragedy.
I take the point: beware. Clots can, keep doing,
and infection knows the best place.

In a street, in the dark, under gaslights at 2 a.m.—
Those 19th-century engravings, low voices.

I Saw a House, a Field

Most of the rooms muted by cold,
and the furniture there
with its human chill under vast drapes
of plastic for the season—

Because eventually we are
an austerity, walking room to room
enamored and saddened, all the crazy variations
of bed and table, clocks,
books on a shelf, foreign harbors etched
some yesterday, framed for a wall.
And the effrontery of windows assuming
how lovely out, a certainty
of lawn and woods, distance on a road, voices
that in summer drift up and move away.

Desire. That continues
and continuing is the part loved
just as there is emptiness with an occasion in it,
clothes to remove before you ease into a bath.

Branches and branches scraping is
winter. And after midnight, near morning when
I stepped out, the moon by half,
was it deer I saw? A little one and maybe
its mother. Or they were
smaller than deer. Or larger.

Oh but they were strange, stopped
across the snow like that.

What do you think?

OUR MISSION:

Poetry is vital to language and living. Copper Canyon Press publishes extraordinary poetry from around the world to engage the imaginations and intellects of readers.

Thank you for your thoughts!

BOOK TITLE: _____

COMMENTS: _____

_____

_____

Can we quote you? ☐ yes ☐ no

☐ Please send me a catalog full of poems and email news on forthcoming titles, readings, and poetry events.

☐ Please send me information on becoming a patron of Copper Canyon Press.

NAME: _____

ADDRESS: _____

CITY: _____ STATE: _____ ZIP: _____

EMAIL: _____

 **Copper Canyon Press**

A nonprofit publisher dedicated to poetry

MAIL THIS CARD, SHARE YOUR COMMENTS ON FACEBOOK OR TWITTER, OR EMAIL POETRY@COPPERCANYONPRESS.ORG

CopperCanyonPress.org

BUSINESS REPLY MAIL
FIRST-CLASS MAIL   PERMIT NO. 43   PORT TOWNSEND WA

POSTAGE WILL BE PAID BY ADDRESSEE

Copper Canyon Press
PO Box 271
Port Townsend, WA 98368-9931

NO POSTAGE
NECESSARY
IF MAILED
IN THE
UNITED STATES

The No-Name Tapestries

When I think of the dead, it means
they're thinking
of me, I delude myself happily, on occasion,
assuming the past

a thing to cherish like a face
surprised I bothered to come at all, given
the rain and the long drive.

But you were always *let's go anyway*.

The commonest phrase: alive and well.
As if we jumped out of a hole
to stand here radiant.

In the no-name old tapestries, many
with halos, a glow or
a circle of jagged lines around each head
never bowed at the table, simply
looking straight on, like a mirror gives us
back to ourselves.

If sometimes the women
in those lush hangings so plainly dressed,
their rims woven
deep and lit, turn sideways, the hills,
a blue distance involved—

Out there. The one vanished, or just now
walking away—

In Dürer's Engraving

Adam gets three for his privates—a triplet affair
as in poison ivy, as in the venerable
box elder. Eve, one wide leaf,
or it could be a smashed, very sorry rose. I need
better glasses. Engravings
take time. Still Adam looks at her—
curious or just wary, was love
invented yet?—and she, only at the snake wrapped
sensibly for balance around a young tree.
An apple. Sure, *the* apple:
okay tempting enough, even as E and A stand there
fully bodied and souled, not terribly young, years
to build up such muscle (Adam), such flesh (Eve) though
I can't say they're long in the tooth. Nary a tooth
to scare that garden. The rumor: no weapons, no way.
Those creatures in the foreground or behind
oblivious, or bored with the notion *prey* in whatever
shaft of light for naps: a mouse, a cat,
an ox, etcetera, each different-dreaming day or night if any
beyond the likes of us really do dream. Curly hair (Eve
with her lots more), side by side, roughly same
height, breadth, the standard
wedding pose—minus outfits—except
between them the snake so soon to be famous
I almost forget Eve's set there to
take her bite. Hunger's urgent echoing no end-to-it,
but whose, and for what...
Because Dürer is a tad ambiguous.
Maybe the snake's merely
a snake famished at this point, mouth
wide open at, on that apple
right out of Eve's hand. And she's not generous,
or just can't imagine—
and will not not not release. Maybe that's
the bloody thorn of it.
No sound in the garden. And closer, so much
weirdity to love. Which one, Adam
or Eve smarter, more full of wanting, of bravado,
wonder, all grief finally but first
able to talk those animals into lounging about,
no vengeance, no tricks, assuming
chats with a snake don't count. I'm not sure what counts.
Or who's even counting though the parrot

(a parrot? large, strange in that setting, a so-what-if-
history-begins-as-some-mythic-dire-reboot
all over him) looks away, in profile, ready to lament not yet
the again again
calm enough on a branch held high by
the first man. Now just a distance,
an apple to take or to give.
It's those was-and-will-be stories my whole life
with a fuck-up inside. Starting sweet,
out of place. Pre-unbearable.

The Professor of Antiquities

Concerning the lost and so
much of it, the Professor of Antiquities
is on TV again—

Think about that.

I love the word *oxymoron* like I love the word
hope loving him back such a long way.

The Ancients then, via digital pulse. But never
to know except with shovel, brush,
magnifying glass. He dreams out the rest.

The rest is resting in dust. The rest too will

come out of deep down—
petrified wood or gold or bronze
fierce, the spear end of it.

So many winged creatures
sculpted out of flight to peer from a ledge,
their grim human heads turned sideways, desert
a distance, a horizon. Column after column
holding up ago

what made it cool in there, made us all
the first days of the world: lie down,
close your eyes a moment,
listen to the fountain.

The Professor of Antiquities
looks into the camera as into what the Oracle saw
and says *you don't destroy,*
you restore. All this time to recover
words for beer, for how-much-you-owe-me, for gods
and king, the body living or in death, what to do,
what's elegy and next
marked on clay tablets with a stick.

First lost layer of city. Shock-seizure
of flames larger than night
after night some year BC burning back
temple or palace until

safe all words, *safe*,
slow-fired to stone in the lower chamber
when everything, everything else—

Vermeer's *Woman In Blue Reading a Letter* on Loan in America

You have mail! beams the exhibit into
witty. Those curators. It could be the newest
among them: *yes, let's!*
What a welcoming principle, humor.

Three and a half centuries staring straight down
that woman keeps reading, no ear
for puns, for such lightness of being. Or she's
being itself ever after. Which
is blue—blue dress,
blue chair at the serious ready.

Across the way the museum's also
a coffee shop, the scent
from Brazil, from Tanzania near Kilimanjaro,
the sound of grinding, a mountainous
delicate dreaming foam-making machine.

Nothing stops her search
for something. Hearts could break or mend
however badly as she reads, tiny
valves doing their best,
the blood flow. Yours. Mine.

Art can be weirdly
instant, not artifice at all, the light
in her room the ordinary same endless

as in our rooms. And is it even thinking,
what we think.

The Offering

Did you kill me or did I kill you?
Jorge Luis Borges, from "Legend"

Cain. Or maybe Abel blurting that out.
And the off-hand question
hangs between them, in whatever

heaven according to hope
and surprise. The shock, reading that
when young, when I read like

never again. Like a good death arrives
in the middle of sleep's
harrowing dark for—o pioneer! old and adrift

inside your slapdash cabin on the prairie, 1833.
And centuries before, great kingdoms
on rivers, up on bluffs

behind walls of skins, of bark,
how they sweetened wolves into
dogs to lie down and warm children,

the sick, the bent
old ones out of their heads, those who
carved boats, knew stars, gave birth.

Spring is birdsong, lush
leafy riot, a jolt: yay!
What a relief the end's not

ice, no snow-smothering-snow to
that's it, pal,
over and done except it wasn't that

great, certain ancient of details give
pause: a burnt sacrifice, the who
next given abruptly

to flames, just in case—
sure, okay—gods invented
on the other side most

duly pleased by the stench
of that burning, to be thanked for
spring, greenery, growth,

any and all beloveds, those lost
and yet to be. The gods
so needy after

that other work, coming up
with outer space and Earth, fabulous
color schemes, not to mention

the astonishing iridescent
northern flicker on a branch—
a visitation, a sudden dumbfounding.

Did you kill me or did I kill you?
And maybe the future does lie
in forgetting, a moment of

some afterlife and shrug,
old enemies settled down at a campsite,
that they do

heat up beans, break off bread, offer
what's left of the eternal to each other.
Probably not love, more

a simple shared exhaustion,
better a break in the cloud: look up,
stay put…   *Don't.*

That's the ant hours ago spelling it
out for me, my hand raised, ready to spring,
her slow dash across the table.

Genuine Fakes

the docent said, pointing to a wall. Paintings and drawings
someone figured would do.

It makes a life, I thought, this redoing what
not that long ago some great, almost-to-great someone did.
It passes the time. And certain ways
with eye and brush and pencil deserve a resurrection.

Beauty is such a crap shoot. And repetition replays
the sun again, *whatever.* The gung-ho illusion
that it rises. Of course weather makes a difference, rain
or snow the wee hours just before
where the moon might be. And if Orion is back
from that other hemisphere
tilting, perpetually amazed his dog's reduced to a star.

The human genius of reproducing not quite exactly.
What outrageous lengths taken, making paint from a new tube
look old—or raising children, for that matter.
He heats up a hot plate in an old pigsty or a garage
off an ordinary suburban yard, a mess of mad
chemistry going on, the forger wearing goggles like
pilots on airmail stamps from the twenties fly
straight into clouds as any artist would,
dreaming of Caravaggio.

Weren't our genes stamped out mostly
again and again the same when our parents by accident or design
lay down after the argument? Until it took.
The usual translation: two arms, two legs. I've been told
I look like my mother, a thing neither of us
much believed.

I don't know. Pick up a pen and those hundreds of
dull and ravishing words
used to death flood back. Honor everything.
And shred and merge and burn.

The Anti-Grief

Day after day of rain. A ticket straight to
the mild-mannered hell of rethinking whatever,

the drive to EconoFoods: not a lot of grief in that.
You need staples—bread, rice, eggs.
Here's a list: almonds, yogurt, all the little
anti-griefs add up.

Did I tell you? my grandfather sings from the grave.
They have my old Philco here.
I know all about your world of god-awful and too bad.

I keep driving. In rain. Some luck required. Stoplight.
Flashy cars on both sides playing radios too loud.
Ear damage! I used to shout out the window,
my boy in the front seat trying hard to shrink, not to know
who *is* that crazy at the wheel.

Grandfather likes saying: what? Half-deaf even now.

Half a lot of things, anytime. Half, what gives?
giving way. If there is a we or a you or an I finally.
He'd cup an ear if he had an ear.

So it is, the first anti-grief, a feather he picked up.
My childhood, walking with
the oldest man I ever, 1874 his
start date. Alarm and Should Have, two roads
he would not cross, and Consequence
a street over, he ignored completely. Always
an eye out for the great
small peculiar.

A feather. Sometimes handed to me. Or he'd
oil a clock with it right off the curb.
Into a pocket.

Back Back

This what they call a blur? That's it?
the blind woman is said
to have said—her sight restored,
who could see

only a color wheel spinning.

To know the blurred thing is to know
what is exact.

We've all been dizzy, gotten up quick
from a metal bench and blinked into traffic.
We've all witnessed a bird
or squirrel drunk on berries wrinkled as peas
spilled in a cellar and left there.

Just so,
just how bird or squirrel = prophet

nails things, and blithely staggers.

I get that none of us outlasts a Roman ruin
or a hideous brocade napkin though
exceptions, yes. We all have
such a someone who flunked hospice,

a *persistant* gone pro, shrugging off our grief.

In that room with no window, who really said
what next she said, who in her or of her
red   green   blue   yellow   *here all this time*—

come back from the dead with one eye,
another to spare.

That Angel William Blake Kept Talking To

He meant Michelangelo's favorite model for his
frescos called down

those many times to strike poses in
too much sunlight and old cathedrals new—

Look sideways to slip
the gauzy afternoon even more

out of focus. To the point
and blinding of Blake, bringing up

the devil he saw too.
Under a grate in London's

coal-sickened air, a seething
monster, *devil* a name for

the worst things. Because his
I can look into

a knot of wood until it frightens me.
But there's rage in the mix

going silver out of kindness.
Once so furious at the father who

tied his son's leg to a log
and made him walk, Blake

roared to the street, spit
lightning all over the man.

Hold that for two centuries.
Not long to

love such a thing
across the gene pool

when any world ends.

The Ache

Every wooden chair a tree one time,
the way night turns day and day turns night.
So I can sit here, pretend nest or kite

in the *branches* of a perfect Windsor
or this kitchen stool I dragged outside.
And wait for leaves to fall

and consider an acorn's
presumption: to be that big!
Or tell you of the treeless spot

I watched little planes circling the smallest
airport, an airport
with a library in it, a lot of

levitation stamped onto pages by those who
ached past cloud, mountain,
all the pretty debris in the offing

on the way to someplace else.
I saw Amelia Earhart there,
climbing into her

deathtrap. But she didn't
know yet, did she? Writing her book
about staying still. I mean flying

which means stuck in one place, glommed
onto knobs and dials and a window
with changeable scenery, the blue vast

Pacific to come, islands, low oxygen to
arrive as vertigo, the works.
I've seen photographs and I like her

so much already. Smart, bobbed-hair-wily
and grinning, gamely walking through
old footage. She could almost be

one of us, you said, a regular wiseass except
she knows things. Would she
come to supper, talk offhand of favorite disasters,

the wretched state of the world and so on?
And leave her flight jacket
behind on a chair. After all, a chair

sprung from an ancestral tree, they have things
in common: passion, delusion, hope,
and winds that throw everything off course,

take down even oaks.
It *is* a big deal, any new life. Behind glass
her cigarette case, silver,

her long silk scarf pale enough,
the very one they took to the moon
and brought back.

Because the moon didn't want it.
The moon indifferent, so *so-what* now
after eons trying to

kick the habit of love and its double,
outright lunacy, all night
staring down.

The Underworld

I watch the little weasel rise just partly
out of a cleft in earth, its face
a periscope at sea, this way and that but not slow as
an owl does it, the moon behind him
in old children's books, his giant tufted head
turning full circle and rich with pause.
Because the weasel isn't patient, but all frenzy.
Through weeds another of its kind drags
to that chamber a tiny mouse stilled
by panic or dying or both,
a natural enough progression. Somewhere a cache
deep, for the kill. Days earlier
a tireless gopher dug out that spot, already
sunk to it, throwing off pebbles
and twigs and dirt, vanishing
for more pebbles and twigs and dirt,
up, down, how much and many until—okay,
to kick back, eat roots of grass and low shrubs, the vast
beneath of the planet emptied and narrowed
to below daylight
and nighttime. Now this axis of stealth between
mountain and ocean is
all weasel. When I slept. Or kept doing
whatever vapid thing I do,
bloodswept moment one of them so much
smaller than the gopher must have
twisted its sinew hard, wire-tightened
the breath out of
he who quiet-clawed and toothed
a small depression to
tunnel, to *secret life.* I understand a shriek
of razor tooth is involved. Quick.
At the nape of the neck. Gophers are loners. So that
was that. Free digs! And lunch for a week.
Layer upon layer, story gives way
to story. Don't tell me not
every bit counts. Really it's two points of descent to
the underworld, a few feet apart.
Weasels at both ends disappear, come back
as if sprung.
A link down there, a passage
dark as the brain refuses to know,
then we do.

Museum Footage, 1945

After Chechnya, after Stalin's Bykivnia,
after ISIS, Boko Haram, Qibya, the Killing Fields.
After Tikrit and Wounded Knee, the great
slave uprisings in the South put down relentless.
After the bile keeps coming, words spewed at a podium,
any monster in a drive-by with a spray can—
After, and after how

in that film they keep dragging
body after body skin deep, bone rag, limp-headed,
to toss them doggedly let's-get-this-done into
a pit the size of an Olympic pool,
the sort lifeguards scan
with only zoned-out attention since
everyone in a place like that swims well enough.

After all, they did swim. It's like
swimming, pitched midair up, arms and legs
flung out to abandon, coming down coming down
to others piled high who sleep—
how dare to call it sleep—these deaths
at last a real death. How dare we *after*,
dazed on a bench to watch this.

The unspeakable redundance. British soldiers
force it at gunpoint, those
draggers and hurlers in a kind of uniform too,
Bergen-Belsen I think, stout
grim women mostly, jackets and skirts and little scarves
knotted vaguely natty, wildly bedraggled, holding
a foot or a hand to haphazard the dead
across the weedy lot and not
the next world, just this vast hole dug by—

Always and after, horror has a stand-still
falling forever about it. Wordless patchy film,
this museum next century, this human
repeatedly who we are.

By then a snake
reels up, ready to spring
from a freezing calm. That's the stricken
stabbing question ever after, isn't it?
Which of us, and *in* us.

I hate even to imagine them. *A decent job,*
in wartime, surely the guards
said at first, those women on screen
limping, thrust forward because
of their load. *We lucky things,* they no doubt

flattered each other, such
bread, good butter, roast rabbit, goose liver—
our kitchen and mess separate
from the rabble. And their ricocheted spite at some
straight-from-cities-by-train, *what fine*
woolen coats, ties, perfect gabardine dresses. . .
Hope, a temporary
not-so-bad, each seaside, to mountain air
suitcase in hand.

No, a *grip* in hand. And not
because we called things differently then.
All doom clicks the same
shut, bone-knuckled. After that
how in the bloodied living hell to carry it.

Sleep, It's Just That

the spirit leaves the body on the bed, heartbeat
slowed, breath a predictable,
smallest movement of eye and hand and arm crooked.

The ghost-to-be gets decent practice that way,
no cartwheels to the window, the moon
as usual yawn, sleek-shiny with sun the earth
turns from each evening.

Moon coming into a house not like rain,
not wind through a screen, not like
childhood again, the broken collarbone of it,
the fall down stairs, a shock
before pain hits. The spirit's mesmerized,

light as intruder, a beauty the moon makes
rinsing all things as if
the sock on a chair really does dream a better life,
the shirt left on a hook given
a parade, a homecoming of sorts. Everything,
then everyone, even the wounded
on hard ground briefly
luminous. In some migration camp
a child at midnight facing a tent wall, the moon's
cold warmth, her hand just so
to make a shadow man walk backward.

All the while ordinary, this room, the body
under sheet and blanket, no matter,
no sad hopeful about it. *Enough*
is enough. The spirit
night after night at the window, a glance
toward the bed, baffling

add, subtract,
whether, how long.

Susanna and the Elders

No, there really are
protocols of submission, my longest-running
friend in the world tells me, a noted historian of maps
and chaos, cities back to blood,
to ancient, those tide-battered fleets
seen through a cloud,
then a fever. My friend who brilliant-ups the old wars,
the hard deliberate they do and do
to heads once attached... So I think past
the noisy solace of chickens those
centuries crossing courtyards to children grateful now
for one toy in the briefest childhoods on Earth,
toward boys conscripted as men for murder and revenge,
no choice in the matter. And always
what's done to the private parts of women who
days or for a lifetime refuse—closed eyes—to discuss it,
whatever medieval age we live in.

Protocol, such an elegant word. So *submission*
might pick up grace the way
suffering is framed for the wall, at least a kind of
please, tell the others
in sacred drafty spaces where the old
still pray their rosaries. Sometimes
their lips move.

In Rome, in a certain church, I liked best our gazing rapt
at the Caravaggios though I mixed up
this part: his doing a Susanna at all. Later it seemed
right to get it wrong, my recall where
she never was, so sure he'd brought her out of that gloom
with his deepest cobalt, rose madder a flare.
And the well-off dignified lechers too, who hide and peer
as she bathes oblivious, all beyond-body joy, she
of the secret places standard for the young,
those elders agog in their
sick dream, grave glimmer of brush after brush
marking that window of their pleasure.

You can write it off
as apocryphal, my swearing I saw such a thing.
But under the earth are

tremors and at sea bottom the most horrific-looking fish
show off their battle scars.
Susanna not knowing, but our knowing, private
to public, the past into present as
submission, the future making of that a *protocol*
because history must do its job of
endless awful recording, because mere memory
is clearly finite.

In those churches, they're shrewd
how they light the great paintings. It's funny
then isn't—the dark sudden, a clicking off
every few minutes. No way to see,
as though time itself hasn't started yet, no way
to understand this world until someone works a coin
from a pocket and drops it
into the box on the wall. *For the poor,*
the sign said. And Susanna, wherever she is,
flooded luminous all over again
unaware of her beauty. Or her fate
to be so remembered.

Nocturne

You Bach yourself or Schubert yourself,
light outside in the cabin dark, 11 p.m., Denali

at treeline, the grizzlies still awake
finding berry unto berry, getting larger

for their trouble, enough to
doze all winter. But it's August! And you

Mozart yourself, our bed a concert hall
of one, that wire in your ear to

time out of time as the moon—is there really
a moon this semi-night?—bestows itself

over mountain and tundra.
Bestows! Old word

growing older that finds us later
and late, dear listener

of worlds above river stream
and gravel bar, caribou to hare to crow,

the dot and dash of sheep up there,
an arctic squirrel curious, stopped,

little sentry of the Park Road
reeling up, back—wind

and scent and wolf. This dream
to keep hearing, hour unto hour

sleep, our simple shared
ageless about to.

Women

Dorothy Wordsworth, toothless
at forty. After that I wouldn't sit for
a "miniature" either, some
vagabond artist huckstering door-to-door
with what passed for a camera.

All praise to my old-country grandmother too,
a girl who told no one, the first
menstrual blood running down her leg
between bean row and cabbage, smudged
into dirt with her bare foot. Scared
turns to: will I die?

We all die, said the priest about my mother
but that's in another life.

See? What you write, writes you back. What I find
puts me in the flames of hell
all over again grateful
or in that first backyard of weeds and brave grass,
some ivy weaving a wall.

Dorothy. With or without her brother—*miles*
the nosy ones tisked—into hills beyond Grasmere
like all English poets packed their fame-to-be
next to lunch in a knapsack and went up.
At least she tended her home lilies too,
her wood sorrel, her violets, they untisked.
As for those wily daffodils
in her journal that "tossed & reeled & danced,"
ones that brother later *mine all mine*—
Right. The old story.

Back to my *busia*, who finally told
her mother during the second bout, the next month
out in fields they'd never own. It's just
the bloody thing kept happening.

Pretty soon you get
a rag between your legs. Pretty soon teeth tire of
the whole business, grinding supper
to bits that go

easier down. But gums get like rock, the mouth
more secret.
Beauty then? The big deal about beauty?

I don't know, says Dorothy Wordsworth, walk around.

The Undoing

Not that creep coming up the stairs I dreamt,
the house empty except for me one night.

Just CNN early evening, some
ordinary good guy, the admittedly
little he knew of bandaging and blood roiling.
To work on, to work through, *press here, stanch the flow*—
A small boy on a pallet now, no sound
in the desert except the shriek
and wail of a mother leaping out of her veil like
an angel to pull him back.

No, don't pretty things up, don't embellish, don't make
more of this than it is. But a given: I hear
worse and worse. Out there in the great world
in the eye of my TV, no nuance or shade, not one tree in sight.

Then what. That creep I dream coming up the stairs,
I rewind him out the door, back into his car, off
under whatever rock. There are
certain powers one longs for.

Like I can lie awake, think of that exhausted
make-do medic, his stethoscope a talisman at heart
between him and every evil eye, a charm
to keep madness on pause. *Yeah, I've been changed by this.*
Even one kid. But so many since
coming here. Not crossfire. Those snipers aim
at the head.

I run that again. And beg the no-hope in me
for one *possible, if only,* a *should,*
bloodless undo, undo. . .

No Names or Lost World or the Most

sacred singular *so preposterous*. . .

One grows old. I know that.
And the thing about *old*—some curl into a box to sleep.
Some have a second life, not dreaming anymore.

The streetlight's gauzy through curtains,
thin as skin stretched to a drumhead.
What is more exact and forgetful than a drum
about to undrum?

The human machinery knows what I'll never,
openings and closings, the valve work,
a buzzing so faint, a catch in the throat and why.

O vigil somewhere, the wish to make
a lot of noise equals a future, equals *I promise.*

I get it, I promise.

Rain on a roof is another and another,
the end of time rattling around up there.

Those few handfuls of string it takes to clog
a riverbed all night, cold currents under and through,
distant traffic, broken branches. . .

The Octopus

fragile. Enraged.
Or terrified at the touch, pulling back,

given the no-room in there, rock
on three sides, out of bay and sun,
low tide Alaska near Homer.

So hallucinate high tide where all of it

floats the life of free water
released, let go, soft underbelly of leathery
sea stars twisting how Picasso
did his nudes crazy-pitched in bad dream.

I'm told the world goes under to nothing it was.

The octopus sees us as shadow, feels us as
feelers, the octopus
wraps and wraps in there, all arms and too many.

A hole, a rock wherein lies an eye, of sorts.

Think the moment the octopus found
this place to tangle up.
Think: fear means a desperate
solace somewhere, like—

until *like* is a hook, a click
to the past wired up as right now
out of whole cloth ago,

the accident that time, the wait
in the car's swollen dark...

And I pictured my bed, my bed, my bed.

To Be in Conversation, He Says, With

Henry James of course. I'm asked at dinner if I too

have read *The Jolly Corner,* the best, a marvel, no question.
Me, stunned by how many
stories that novelist wrote, including this
of the ridiculous title, Henry James not such a jolly guy
to my mind. But I get it's a ghost tale.

I love this though. I love that the rug in this room
could be thought
in conversation with the floor and wall and window.
What about exhaustion, boots dragging in
a now-microscopic recall
of dog shit and sand from the beach.
I remind myself, not sadly: no beach around here
and besides, it's winter.

In conversation. The back-and-forth between
stars and planets, Cassiopeia stuck crooked in her chair,
singing out her bad bones to the void.

Down where we are, who wouldn't
want to be *in conversation* with the rare
salt-of-the-earth who trusts each day to keep on
okay enough to bear, or if not,
well, not...

And what would it mean to look
at a glass of wine as if
in conversation with grapes, rain, sun,
at least three languages
tangled up there, the sweat, the old relief

of lunch before the long afternoon
wears out. Then it grows
dark in those vineyards, and whatever's sacred
about worms and sparrows

beds down too. And all talk stops.

Aubade in Spring

The soft rattle, then pause
of the _____ (note to self: check
the bird tapes) is like it's
a breathing. I pace mine to match.

This and *early* in the same brain scan
make it so private, the *this*
a Rorschach test: the who am I really, a blip
among the names of things that circle
and nest at daybreak.

It's *turn over a new leaf* every
whitherwhere, for real. If I were a poet
I'd say *but I am a poet.*

Which comes first: the god of forgetting
or the god remembering stupid things like that—

My heart plays
dangerous with me, doing cartwheels, a trick
I never learned in childhood,
other kids upside-down-whirling
lawn ornaments aglitter, each
part on the fly.

Darkening fog, you could lift…

Θ

There Ought to Be a Law against Henry

given his showing up to teach at the U
disheveled, jittery cigarette and cigarette and probably
the drink, losing the very way there
over river, river of all song, all-American story
which starts way north of St. Paul quiet or undone
wandering south, not
enraged mostly, something stranger.
That's one epic shard of John Berryman anyway.

Notorious. And par for the course in a classroom
destined, struck by lightning
in sacred retrospect, the kind those long-ago students
now can't believe themselves
so accidently chosen, grateful though one
probably claimed the poet absolutely
bonkers then, *out of his tree* toward the end,
so went the parlance. Wasn't he
always late—*Give them back, Weirdo!*—with those
brilliant papers they eked out, small dim-lit
hours when a big fat beer would've
been nice. Really nice.
Fuck him, I hear that kid most definitely
blurting were he young right now
though the others—— From the get-go their
startle and reverence. But not even that malcontent
did the damning *I can't believe*
they gave him tenure.

Here's where I think something else, think
of course it's the *Dream Songs* that rattled him until—
as grandparents used to say—he couldn't
see straight. Like Dickinson's bits of shock and light
did her in between naps and those letters to
some vague beloved unattainable. Or Plath, her
meticulous crushing fog. Maybe closer to Milton working
his blindness—literally blind rage, if you want
to talk rage—into pages soaked through with triumphant
failure and rhyme, always
that high orchestration, that alpha/omega big voice thing.
And Satan, after all, as wise guy
and looming because *for chrissake, Jack, get an interesting*
character in there! Someone must have
lobbed that right.

All along, Berryman: how those *Dream Songs* surely
loosened a bolt or a wheel in his orderly
scholar-head, must have come at him
like Michael the Archangel, seventy-seven days of winged flash
searing him to genius, some kind of
whack-a-mole version. Maybe like Gabriel
cutting that starry celebrity deal
for a most dubious conception in the desert, near a fig tree,
no proper human mechanics required. At last
Berryman's rage wasn't rage
but sorrow turned back on itself. With teeth.

Henry my hero of crankiness and feigned indifference,
unspeakable industry, exhaustion
and grief, half funny-crazy, half who-knows-what-
that-line-means. A henry whole
universe of Henry, of
there ought to be a law against Henry—pause
and pause—*Mister Bones: there is.*
Will be! Was! Not to say poetry's
worth it or the most healthy fascination for the sane.
I'm just, I mean—is this love?

There's *break* as in lucky, as in
shatter. There's *smitten* and there's *smite.*

All of Us All of Us

Anyone could stand in a kitchen, tiny
barbs of arrow sinking
in again. Whoever shot it good
missed the heart.

That's the problem, isn't it?   The only partly.
Brave and pathetic the way we
walk away okay enough, and think things.

Something fated to be given, but not gotten.
Something dreamt never coming with, on waking.
No longer no longer no longer something.

It's the repeat—how a car
can drive the same road home, years
the ruts, the standing water every spring.
It can make you sick because
you wanted to love it.

To keep the already said going,
to sit then rise again. And to
leave in the sink: the cup with a little coffee,
lettuce on a plate from lunch.
All of us, all of us.
Even anguish in such small things is

everyone singing.

On Halos

More halos than these days.

Something understood: keep the dark
a little distant, plus a stab at marking, a *Who's Who*
of unlikely star-studded beings.

Such old paintings. And the lucky ones—
Are they lucky? Past human or pre-human
lit that way, sitting intent enough where
going blank could equal patience, tables piled
with bread, goblets of shade.
Or they stand around lush courtyards. And beyond,
what deserts offer up—
one tree, a few leaves, a lot of expanse
drifting off into that vague horizon I've heard
plenty about. Oil paint takes months,
years to dry out. To be
means to wait and to wait.

The artist's work, the real work—
those orbits each time depending on
faces, the ones
who watch, the ones about to speak what's never
been said or it's the knee-jerk song
and story. Confess. Maybe not murder,
not that particular seizing up. But a low-grade
alarm or ecstasy in some.

Halos keep haloing. Zigzags or
simple circles, a luminous wisp pulled constant,
to curve. Or a plate pure
shiny gold behind each head like
cardboard cut and sprayed from a can for
a really dumb school project.

The painters aren't reverent. Better, they're
earnest and love the outrageous
layers of things. A halo: to see in the dark
and be perfect, a standard
miraculous skill right up there with—

Pick one: flying through clouds, arms

straight out past stray birds thinking you're
the lunatic, or going invisible
in a crowd of the jubilant, the depressed, the mean,
the sweet, the relentlessly self-absorbed.
Then there's talking with animals again, having
that conversation I like
to have with them about the end of everything—
the planet, the slow
afternoon going nowhere.

Brushstroke. Brushstroke. . .

And what would a cat do but
curl up in the usual
medieval pool of light. Probably on a bed.

What to Know on a Need-to-Know Basis

First and for decades
sandstone   marble   granite.

This last, by the way, you position
hammer and chisel head-on, lunge all you got
though with sandstone it's
a shallow business, any old angle vs.
the 45 degrees marble begs for release.

So a certain sculptor told me.

Cutting rock, I thought, a rare medieval
pain in the ass but what a rush
joining the great work of figuring
all of it back to the original moment,

a terrible banging,

mostly gravel and dust, the human take
on the hard miraculous when they made angel
after angel look like
anyone through a window, rapt luminous
before a blue TV. Or like so many
streetwise at dusk with wings
tucked back, pitched into their lit handhelds.

Even the young have years of

triumph and loss and make-do
in their grit. Just wait. But really, the time
it takes, his wife's clothes not
given away, in the closet months, and for nothing,
that fist-around-a-mallet thing: up, let down,
break and fall, how to

chip away   burnish   find a mirror in it...

Whatever intricate expletive
needed, cigarette after cigarette, smoke-swirl
a vigil, an offering to the next day,

and grief, made of stone too.

Plenty of that around, the kind that
gives way quick.
Or it's the stubborn granite

taking every blow, to face straight.

Incant Until Gone

that room that room that room—

His desk as upright piano, minus music.
His many cubbies once you flipped the lid up.
Razor blades and cotton balls with flecks of old blood.
Bottles of salves, cloudy elixirs, his truss on a hook.

The chiming clock mainly, largely.

A shadowed cove of a room when
he slept on the daybed downstairs and—
flip a coin—the losing kid
got it on visits.

Because sleeping in that bed alone
you needed a paddle to reach

the moonless places, ducking branches, owls
so hungry their heads spun around.
And trains in the narrow between fields
sounding night into far.

I lie down after dark in my own house
to know nothing again. Stains on his wall—

that room that room that room—

an almost human in a nightshirt with a candle who
never sleeps either, look-alike ordinary,
blurred sort-of and kind-of...

Justice and Mercy

O bad dream of email announcing straightaway
another dream: *do not open this.*

I stayed back for a day thinking
it fell across the screen like a veil.

Because there is neither mercy nor justice,
my friend's cells go haywire in the pancreas

sweeping the room of ordinary chitchat.
What can one say? one says and says like

a circle or a brick. Did I finally? Open, I mean.
I mean it can't mean that.

Consider how even a lousy lowly virus
spellbinds and draws in the body like

a shaman rearing up before fire as
wolf and tooth, classic

cave drawings wheeling above into
crooked constellations, someone at them once,

oblivious as hope upon hope, steady,
wild to finish, stained by

hardcore mystery: *how   to   do   this.*
A woman told me women most likely, new facts

about the width of the bare-minimum hurried
handprints there. Hand as stencil flat to the wall

to stop time, red ochre blown through
reed or bone. A blue mash too, I'm guessing.

Watch her grind the daylights out of
the weirdest looking roots, add

spit and fat and blood to make things stick.
How did we get here all the way

from the Ice Age, convinced
we'd never end. *Do not* and *Open*

don't belong in the same sentence.
Are words portals or
bent backs to carry outer space home,
a shroud that only

gets heavier. It's not right.
And so 21st century to say so.

Hospital Linens

They take the linens every day, the bloody linens
worn through by sweat
and sleeplessness. Simple bleach at the end of it,
soap swirling itself gray-green, huge washers
shudder and stop, the sound of
planes landing.

Not just surgeries. It's mainly
ordinary seepage, the drip down tubes into arms,
drains in secret to abdomen
and lung. Always sheets bearing up their cool finish
as if nothing will happen, then caught in
that lie. The life behind fabric—cotton, flax
in the weave—is a seed broken,
getting ahead of itself by tiny increments
unwatchable because we
have no patience with the slower inscrutables.

A woman drives this morning, takes the linens out
one door to the street and into another.
Huge plastic bags encloud her, dizzy her, sicken
bird-whirl her. Bedazzlement keeps
staining, the dry brush-by of
so many wings. She has a hard time with balance.

Nothing to make of it, nothing but
look again. The bloody linens, evidence.
And the little truck they drive
not much more than
a go-kart really, a runabout.

Speak to Me

Stephen busy raising six people from the dead.
All in a day's work. Or those saints
who carry what killed them, a sort of totem, loving
the fragrance. Lawrence, for one, dragging
the smoked gridiron he roasted on.

So goes fate in this life, stop-action
squares of it at the museum. Or in an oval
there in St. Louis, that
Smiling Girl, a Courtesan, Holding an Obscene Image,
a medallion of a nude, inscription
from the Dutch: *who can tell my backside from behind?*
What some rich merchant showed someone
in secret, 1625, no doubt sick
with lust, the both of them out and about one afternoon
to see the heretic not flayed,
not hung upside down anymore.
Still, what a crowd in the street. Good times.

The body has its business. Even the lesser arts
do its bidding. I admit being charmed by
a handle disguised as a rose on
Emily Dickinson's chamber pot, itself
a thinnest blue porcelain, corner of her room in Amherst
facing a busy road. Busier now. No matter.
I heard she wrote at night.

Saint John in his painting, 4th century, must know
a dark thing or two. *The mouth's downward curve
and the echoing arc of his brow tell us
the saint's in distress.* So a curator, a curator...

I want to say *dreams.* Because John's intact,
a regular guy in this one though soon,
minus the rest of him, his head only and alone.
Its permanent last address
was a platter.
Human hands to do that job. Of course. And hands
to hold the plate.

One learns such things, staring down.
Third grade. Walking home across the playground.

A holy card given us before Easter's all
chocolate and eggs dyed
the most garish colors. Oh raging

hair of him, flung furious
open mouth—

Divers on Film

In real life they mainly
danger and disappear, no big deal
standing poised
over the blue drop, arms out high at
world's edge, holding back—
not to tempt the dark nothing, still
a kind of surrender that
five, six seconds the human heart's
compacted, then down

of course, straight down

given gravity's deathless insistence.
Yet at poolside a camera
aimed under that blue exactly where
the forever-after
aftermaths and breaks,

body a thing

shot, split-second rush
to the bottom so
slo-mo now, on film. Vast foaming
fills the screen at the wall

instant for replay the white mess
of our going gone wayward
rising rivulets of cloud—

I swear a cloud—

as body arrows up, unarms,
escapes the fire it makes
of water each time, a cold searing
in plain sight

the smoke of us, any
love and fear once.

A Firmament

To remember. Because we don't do that
quite right in America. Edinburgh! Where impatience
wore down patience, our waiting in rain or the about
to rain. But a lull between darkest sky and shiny
moss-glorious trees, whatever wild neglected garden
seen from the street, my favorite kind of beauty.

Enough said, I guess. All the alas and whatnot
in that city. A few graves, an iron gate
as we stood there, and our bus
flares up, stops, wheezing open near an old
was-it-a-church? Same late afternoon
same sepia, stones mortared with smaller stones to
finish a wall in gloom so far
gone ago. The ordinary *is* strange—
duh!—a mash-up.
Zone *then*. Zone *now*. Zone *everlasting*. Any century
workmen calling it quits, stalking off
for a pint and bangers and mash, more of this world
than sorrow.

Well. Which is to say we were
up that double-decker in a flash, at one with mouthy
punks lip-pierced, at one
with the oldest, most elegantly scarved ladies
buttoned up to the throat. Home to
supper like everyone else,
time travel and lens. Sweet damn!
be damned.

I wish a specific corner came to mind but the months
and months since have their own blank and vivid
business to forget.
It's gone or I'm gone, we were or never were
is the thing.

The place I mean might be
just down from Waverley or closer to the flat
on Strathearn, a kitchen we loved, our pull on the rope
until laundry filled the upper quadrant of the room, and behind
a sprawl of shirts and socks strung up to dry, we stared out

distant, that observatory, that hill: *we should*
go sometime. Starry bits named or not and which ones...
Light years burn up there.

A gate, a street, a shrug, wide lull in the heavens.
And future past—
a verb tense to be invented yet.

Light in Winter

The door wide as a gurney—

those in scrubs at the side,
all fluids on hooks—

a real thing, not
the happenstance drift of a thing.
Which is to say I don't own it. I don't.

Or this freezing day—

I stare too long at anything. A crack in the wall,
a paint drip that looks
like a hand offering up a smallness, a quiet.
Light muted for months, framed
window-as-conduit, a go-between.
Every night some creature does
intricate absolutions between
plaster and struts. It doesn't take long.
Or I fall, fall asleep.

Plain cloth stretched for the easel.
Because how many painters ran low on color
in their kit, the slightest
shade of dawn to it. And loving that cold nothing
asked a bare strip of canvas to blunt-edge
through woods. Lie down, please,
be a road all this distance
from a fireball.

A door narrows
to the gurney. It must be winter, my

thinking such things.

The Carnivorous Plants

in exile, ganged up in this greenhouse of living ache
and want, shabby glassed-in room with a door
propped open under a scribbled *please, keep locked*
underlined times two. Who wrote that, what

guardian of the wordless deep to
abet these bullies on their bright mottled stalks
breathing in my carbon, giving back
oxygen. The invisible exchange—love that first.

But trays and trays of dirt growing miniature time bombs,
tiny eyelids with a clamshell look, eyelashes if
brushed even slightly, they go for me. One clamps up
quick as I pull away. I'm its *feed me right now,* I'm prey

then a total wash-out, too big for its little, a tease.
Slowly it reopens, on watch over this ocean of
sunlit muggy air, me swimming through my so important
afternoon to supper, to sleep. What to dream at night—

who knows how ruthless a small empty creature can be
to swallow anything that happens by, to give it
an afterworld, a shot, a slow dissolve.
I have eyelids. I have lashes that shut down tight.

Once a Procession

More like seawash or insects louder by such
small increments I couldn't even think
how many—and huge that church in Rome,

vast nave, every lost kingdom on earth I confused,
my straining to their muted cloud coming, who
and so slow, that they walked, they walked,

a migration! (to flee, to abandon, to breathe,
to land somewhere seasick and finally),
same sticks and stones sounding out of them,

a mantra rubbed back so far only the forgotten
first gods might know the exact duration,
two, three notes, layer on layer paused the way

the moon is always misery and beauty at odds,
precise as a clock strikes and closer, faces
empty with light, tearing up or already

shattered, a few in alb and chasuble, the long line,
five pilgrims across, the young and those in between—
maybe two hundred—even the old

in a dim last wish, a whole village I guess
with a steeple, a bridge, a river
winding through grass and potatoes and rye,

all drawn *toward*, synchronized
after a fashion to work time to what-is-time,
haunted no thought until every thought.

The Rings of Saturn

Those ladies at the rummage sale
have buried bodies they love. I believe that
though who could guess,
the way they joke and count: out of a twenty
that leaves ten, or would you
care for a five, a few ones, a little change?

Yes, that would be great.
But he stopped breathing midafternoon
almost three years ago or
she never felt all that well after her fall down the stairs.
Therefore, it ends. It does. And here comes

the donation of ties he liked best, extra wide
to leave room for the jubilant serious
dogs playing cards on them, shooting pool, sitting down
to crack hard-boiled eggs, drink beer.
What a country, isn't it? she of apron and button-up tells
her compatriots shaking their heads,
the standard drill among those who run
rummage sales. Mark my words, says another,
whoever buys one of these
buys all of these.

Friend, make of it while you can
what you can.

If there's really a moment for truth, it will never include
a confession of the crap I bought.
I'm here to point out
back in the corner called *Thrifty*—two dollars a bag—
shirts assigned to orbit
on a circular rack. I spin and move it along like
a *beam me up* space station
into a nothingness so far above Earth, the rings of Saturn
flash their nothing yellows, nothing blues
beautiful. Pure vapor.

Keats Is Coughing

Everything is made of everything.
Leonardo, the *Notebooks*

I found Rome in the woods.

Fair to admit it's mostly
tundra to the west in the park, past Toklat
the Denali I revised, low grasslands
engineered to freeze deep
by October—this being Alaska—the great

    Tabularium close to the Temple of
    Castor and Pollux I rebuilt that same summer—
    not superimposed, exact as any scheme

in secret—the Arch of Septimius Severus at the gravel bar
    where fox drank from a river turned stream,
        a Theater of Marcellus near
            the ranger station where one raven,

                    such a brat,
    complained of
            my Circus Maximus, my Trajan's Column,
              my Baths of Diocletian,
too many spots
soaked in unpronounceable Latin.

        I really did, I shouldered bits of it,
    a ruin-hushed haunted business, my brain
              a truck bed, a lift,
pulleys big as a whale's heart,
expletives of cheap wonder all over
            my woodlot
and expanse.
        One self-anoints to embellish
day, years, life thus far, and think oneself so...

        Then busted—
by a raven!

Well, that's memory for you, that's so-called
    civilization for you, to layer up,
        to redo the already done.

I mean it's a fact, the puny lifespan we're allotted.
　　　　And proof—Denali in August, fireweed,
spunky scrawny first Latinate, *Chamerion angustifolium*

　　　　　giving off flowers to mark
　　　　　what weeks left, little
　　　　　time bomber, time traveler, ancient
　　　　　slips red-flagging the countdown to winter
　　　　　by climbing its own stalk.

Something perverse about that.
Something perfectly fiendishly self-conscious about that.

＊ ＊ ＊

From the start perverse, any premise.
　　　　Ask…　　We can't know.　To be compelled

　　　　　makes an occasion.　Rome's grand
　　　　past horrific, fire and ash, swamp or bog, lust
　　　　　and bloodlust—

The Alaska Range dreams lurid as Rome,
　　　　　　　　the worst
underground being fire, summer snow at night
　　　　off the highest peaks by noon
　　　　　　so distant, the size
of a hand if
　　　　　　　I held up the one with
　　　　　　　an eye in the middle to know

how this works.　Some have the power to
raise from the dead a *before, before*
scary and beautiful
　　　　　　back to mystery cults, in caves, rubble
far under a Roman street, the altar to
Mithras still slaying his bull, crumbling the stonework.

　　　　All things being equal.　They're not.
　　　　　　Agony, it's older.
　　　　　　　Ask the moose at Denali,
　　　　　　　　the snowshoe hare, the lynx,

such a wily courtly lot.

Ask Ovid
banished to his hovel on the Black Sea, aching
for Rome's exalted rude cacophony, each
exiled month a big thick X down

Februarius, Aprilis to
the home-shattered sick enough
for an undersong.
Look it up! *Undersong: a strain; a droning;*
the burden of a song—
Maybe that lowest
common denominator is
contagious. Rome or Denali,
a mash-up of lunge and cry out, predator
and prey throwing coins to a fountain,
footholds made first by a hoof,
pickpockets at buses and trains, nuns
queuing up their no-nonsense, brambles thorny,
raggedy spruce groves,
a look, a nod to sell loveless
love on the street, a chain of mountains in
choral repeat, saints
stained to glass, how ice gouged rivers
from rock-bound,
the one-lung rapturous
common-sense pope,
all outstretched arms, his little popemobile circling
the thrilled at St. Peter's
up on our rickety chairs to see in six, seven languages
how radiant—
Cross my heart, he was.
And Keats,
Keats is coughing.

* * *

You find the fossil record everywhere. In woods,

tundra, under streets, in cadaver labs.
Not those bright transparencies,
wistful orderly page after page in
biology a lie, a kind of flip-book romance.
It's the one big mess of us
in us, the generous dead prove that,

81

signing a paper, giving themselves away
                              to be cut, *disembodied* for
the knowing it,
sunk to their chemical depth in some afterlife, opened
on a table by kids really,
                              belabored doctors-to-be, our
shabby shared *wilderness* to untangle,
bones   joints   arteries   valves,
                              The Dissector
in hand, most numbing how-to
on the planet. Ditto Keats, 1819, same book really,
his margin's scribbled roses and sunflowers
ache an elsewhere,
                    his training,
                    his anatomy theater,
looking down and later—
London, then Rome (he who *gets* it,
   body fails, second floor, beside the Spanish Steps)—
                         Heart, not
my heart anymore.
                         Forgive me. I'm worse
than the hopelessly confused misnomer,
English sparrow, descendant of the great weaverbirds
of Africa, a finch that lost the gene

      for *nest,* how *to beneath, to across* intricate, precise
and can't, but keeps bringing
sticks and hair, bits of shiny paper to make and make.
Undersong: the *burden* of a song.
                              Poor bird. Poor sweet
muddled middle of it. I watched
morning after morning, his offering...
                              It's Keats
who made claims about beauty and time.
His bed at the last
              too low for the window, his must-have
              tell me, what's out there—

I admit: a ridiculous layering, this Rome in
that Denali. Just *because?*
Two continents, an ocean apart. My mother
loved hand-me-down expressions—
never the twain shall meet.
They do meet.

To repeat: that's civilization for you.
Happenstance and *this minute* drag along
future and past
                    and why the hell not
the Denali, the Rome in us, no two
states of being more
unalike, worn-out compulsion
to collect and harbor, piece together,

                    stupid into

some remember machine.

   Such fabulous unthinkable inventions we've made
   to merge or unmake: the trash compactor,
   the poem, all tragedy and story, pencils sharpened to

a point that keeps breaking, wilderness gone inward as

            an ocean ship container,
                a Gatling gun,
                    the AR-15 of the seething deranged,
                    the H-bomb,
                        Roman legions
to Canterbury to blood up
fields into legend then dig the first plumbing but

                    *how can you
                    be in two places at once
                    when you're not anywhere at all!*

   (Thank you, Firesign Theatre, brilliant wackos,
        old vinyl on a turntable still in the game…)

        Fine. Fuck it. Start over.

                    * * *

See the sheep on high ledges, the arctic squirrels below.

See the way Dante saw, sweeping his arm across
Vasari's great painting as Boccaccio looks off, the plague
sealing city after city. Dante

in hell, steady-luminous
      those fact-finding trips to service

his worldly *Inferno*, the bad guys.
the good guys.

Winter sleeps *through*.
August at Denali, bears shovel it down
    a razor-edged maw—

                        twigs! berries! more stems!—
Fate hoards to prepare, subzeros, fattens into...

See the Park's camper bus, ninety-two miles of
jolt and slow, crossing
hours more daylight than night all summer,
rattling tin can with its
exhaust and hissing gravel, the fear
landslide,
        an undersong just possible, how we
zigzag a mountain. Look!

              Nearing a bear, the young caribou abruptly
                hesitant, shy as a leaf—

No! Don't! Do not! That grizzly
huge, bent to his ploy *just*

                these berries around here,
his ignore ignore, sure,
quiet-tense as a trigger, and we of
        fogged scratched windows so hard to open—

Stop! The bus stopped. *Jesus.* The thing curious, closer...
    They're not

that smart anyhow, a stage-whispering drunk from the back
    of our imperial realm, mile 62, the Park Road.

What did Venus decree in her temple down whichever
narrow street in Rome, the Ancients'
              stink of slops, standing water,
      a bear chained to a slave (out of *slav,* by the way,
          backdrop is *horde, human spoils*)

both shackled to a grindstone for
                        a later mob and roar.

Here's what we saw: the little caribou
    in reverse wanders sideways and safe.

Our bus one big sigh or

like a wheezing asthmatic
brakes unbrake.

Bad dream, bad dream, the undersong start to all fable if
                    for real we'd seen that kill back
to lions off their continent
cornered, bloodied in the great amphitheaters, rearing up,
a nail to hammer's
                    bite and blow. The wilderness in us

is endless. Near the cabin, near evening, a warbler
                    in the fireweed
                              hawk saw or heard,
                    his switchblade clicked to—
                                        I was and I was
                    whirling feathers, either bird—
    Every hunger
                    is first century. Forever-thus
feral cats at the Forum about to leap too.
                              The Forum, last homage
    I shoveled out rocks to
remake, mile 82, while the haymouse riddled the meadow
down deep, her catacombs.

                    * * *

Time + beauty = ruins. Perfect shapes in the mind

        meet my friends Pointless and Threat and Years of
        Failure to Meld or Put to Rest. Ruthless
                                        is human.

I ask a composer: How to live with this *undersong* thing
                    over and over, how to
                              get rid of it,
                                        rid the world of it—

    He looks to the heavens—*what undersong thing?* And shrugs
        I'll put it on the test. Let students define it!

    So I dreamt such a test: Go there. To Rome.
            Half-doze against a wall
            two thousand years of

flesh sweat insect wing ago, stone laid by hand, by
a boy when a whip, a whip, a welling up, his *will not speak.*

Have at it. Please explain. Please fill in this blank.

Grief punctures like ice, moves like a glacier
    to flat and slog and myth, low blue and white flowers
        we hiked *trail-less.* The rangers insist. They insist—

    never follow or lead, never lay down a path.

                          From above
the look of us spread out, our seven or eight
a band, little
stray exhausted figures
                  over the land bridge from Asia,

circa: prehistory keeps coming, older than Rome,
both both underfoot, understory, underway

    miles below numb, it's burning.

                  * * *

To see at all, you *time*

              and *this time* and *time again.*

The spirit leans
intrigued, the other part bored, then there's *want,*
                then there's *wait.*

Once a city began with a wolf whose two human pups would
    build, would watch it fall, nursing
                at her milk for centuries
      in marble
      in bronze.

      She stands there and cries of
                that pleasure, by turns
a blood-chill. The tundra. At night.

A snake eats its own tail, endlessly at it on a fresco.
A real snake
        leaves his skin near the gravel bar. Some words
sting, some are sung. Another life
isn't smaller.

Acknowledgments

Enormous thanks to the editors of the following publications who first took a chance with these poems, some in a slightly different form: *The American Poetry Review, The Believer, The Cincinnati Review, Crazyhorse*, Denali National Park's *Alpenglow, FIELD, The Georgia Review, The Journal of American Poetry, The Kenyon Review, Narrative, The New Yorker, The New York Review of Books, Ploughshares, Plume, Poetry, River Styx, Volt*, and *West Branch*. And to the editors of anthologies, online or in print, who requested unpublished poems: The Academy of American Poets Poem-a-Day website (editor, Alex Dimitrov) and its Poem-a-Day site (January 2018; editor, Kaveh Akbar), the "Dangerous Women" project at the Institute for Advanced Studies in the Humanities at the University of Edinburgh (former director, Jo Shaw), the Denali National Park's Artist-in-Residence webpage (editor, Jay Elhard), and *Umbrellas of Edinburgh* (editors, Russell Jones and Claire Askew).

Thanks as well to Denali National Park, the American Academy in Rome, Yaddo, the Anderson Center in Red Wing, Minnesota, the MacDowell Colony, and Djerassi for the support and shelter that aided the making of several poems in this book. And to Purdue University, which funded travel to some of those places. Special gratitude to the insightful art historian Roberta Bartoli for her memorable show *Revealing the Body: The Art of Anatomy* at the Minneapolis Institute of Art in 2015, which included Dürer's engraving *Adam and Eve*. Also at the MIA briefly was the Vermeer painting reimagined here, while *Smiling Girl, a Courtesan, Holding an Obscene Image* referenced in "Speak to Me" is at the St. Louis Museum of Art. Gratitude to the staff at the Emily Dickinson House (Amherst, Massachusetts) as well, for the visit to her room which helped give rise to that poem. And I'm also indebted to philosopher Patricia Curd for her comments about ancient Roman and Greek burial habits, tapped in "The Museum of Silence," and to my English Department colleague at Purdue, Marlo David, for her charming great-uncle story borrowed for "Salmon." Continuing warm thoughts for my time in Rome at the Keats House and the American Academy, and for conversations with sculptor Peter Rockwell in that city, while closer to home, gratitude still for the gross human anatomy class (the so-called cadaver lab run by James Walker at the IU Medical School at Purdue), which flooded back to influence "Keats Is Coughing." Also in that poem is a morphing from a phrase that my nephew Aaron Boruch repeatedly said as a toddler when asked dumb questions by grown-ups, his "I can't know." Meanwhile I remain profoundly appreciative for the UK Fulbright at the University of Edinburgh that made possible "A Firmament" and "Women."

Certain poems here are part gift to others—"On Haloes" for Mary Szybist and Jerry Harp, "Nocturne" and "Salmon" for David Dunlap, "Pieces on the Ground" for Will Dunlap, "Back Back" for Tony Hoagland, and "Susanna and the Elders" for Palmira Johnson Brummett.

Once more I am lucky—meaning David and Will Dunlap, their ongoing love and wise counsel. I'm fortunate for others dear and close, especially Eleanor Wilner, whose grace and wry heartening advice often clicked on the light. And for what it's worth, against what is soul-shattering, this book is for—and in loving memory of—brilliant, life-saving poets Brigit Kelly and Lucia Perillo, good friend and good friend, years to cherish.

About the Author

Marianne Boruch's nine previous poetry collections include *Eventually One Dreams the Real Thing* (2016), *Cadaver, Speak* (2014), and *The Book of Hours* (2011), a Kingsley-Tufts Poetry Award winner, all from Copper Canyon Press. She's published a memoir, *The Glimpse Traveler* (Indiana, 2011) about hitchhiking in the early 1970s, and three essay collections on poetry—*In the Blue Pharmacy* (Trinity, 2005), *Poetry's Old Air* and *The Little Death of Self* (Michigan's "Poets on Poetry" series, 1995 and 2016). Her work has appeared in *The American Poetry Review, FIELD, London Review of Books, Narrative, The Nation, The New York Review of Books, The New Yorker, Ploughshares, Poetry*, and elsewhere. Three of her poems have been chosen for *Best American Poetry*; four have received Pushcart Prizes. Twice a National Endowment for the Arts Fellow, Boruch has also been awarded a Guggenheim Fellowship and residencies at the Rockefeller Foundation's Bellagio Center, Yaddo, the MacDowell Colony, the American Academy in Rome, Djerassi, the Anderson Center, Denali, and Isle Royale in the upper end of Lake Superior, our most isolated national park. In 2015, she was given the Indiana Authors Award (national division) by the Glick Foundation. A 2019 Fulbright Senior Lecturer at the International Poetry Studies Institute at the University of Canberra, Australia, and a 2012 Fulbright Professor at the University of Edinburgh, she was the founding director of Purdue University's MFA program in the English department. Having taught there for thirty-two years, Boruch has now gone emeritus though she continues on faculty (since 1988) in the low-residency program for writers at Warren Wilson College. She and her husband, David Dunlap, live in West Lafayette, Indiana, where they raised their son.

Poetry is vital to language and living. Since 1972, Copper Canyon Press has published extraordinary poetry from around the world to engage the imaginations and intellects of readers, writers, booksellers, librarians, teachers, students, and donors.

WE ARE GRATEFUL FOR THE MAJOR SUPPORT PROVIDED BY:

THE PAUL G. ALLEN
FAMILY FOUNDATION

Anonymous

Jill Baker and Jeffrey Bishop

Anne and Geoffrey Barker

Donna and Matt Bellew

John Branch

Diana Broze

The Beatrice R. and Joseph A. Coleman Foundation Inc.

The Currie Family Fund

Laurie and Oskar Eustis

Mimi Gardner Gates

Nancy Gifford

Gull Industries Inc. on behalf of William True

The Trust of Warren A. Gummow

Carolyn and Robert Hedin

Bruce Kahn

Phil Kovacevich and Eric Wechsler

Lakeside Industries Inc.
on behalf of Jeanne Marie Lee

TO LEARN MORE ABOUT UNDERWRITING
COPPER CANYON PRESS TITLES,
PLEASE CALL 360-385-4925 EXT. 103

WE ARE GRATEFUL FOR THE MAJOR SUPPORT PROVIDED BY:

Maureen Lee and Mark Busto
Peter Lewis
Ellie Mathews and Carl Youngmann as The North Press
Hank Meijer
Gregg Orr
Petunia Charitable Fund and adviser Elizabeth Hebert
Gay Phinny
Suzie Rapp and Mark Hamilton
Emily and Dan Raymond
Jill and Bill Ruckelshaus
Cynthia Sears
Kim and Jeff Seely
Richard Swank
Dan Waggoner
Barbara and Charles Wright
Caleb Young as C. Young Creative
The dedicated interns and faithful volunteers
of Copper Canyon Press

The Chinese character for poetry is made up of two parts:
"word" and "temple." It also serves as pressmark for
Copper Canyon Press.

The poems are set in Centaur fonts.
Printed on archival-quality paper.
Book design and composition by Katy Homans.